Bumps, Bruises, and Scrapes

ELAINE LANDAU

Marshall Cavendish
Benchmark
New York

Marshall Cavendish Benchmark
99 White Plains Road
Tarrytown, New York 10591
www.marshallcavendish.us

Expert Reader: Leslie L. Barton, M.D., professor of Pediatrics, University of Arizona College of Medicine,
Tucson, Arizona

Library of Congress Cataloging-in-Publication Data
Landau, Elaine.
  Bumps, bruises, and scrapes / by Elaine Landau.
     p. cm. — (Head-to-toe health)
  Summary: "Provides basic information about minor bumps, bruises, and scrapes, and their prevention"—
Provided by publisher.
  Includes bibliographical references and index.
  ISBN 978-0-7614-2849-7
  1. Children—Wounds and injuries—Juvenile literature. 2. Bruises—Juvenile literature. I. Title. II. Series.

RD93.5.C4L36 2009
617.10083—dc22
2007026959

Editor: Christine Florie
Publisher: Michelle Bisson
Art Director: Anahid Hamparian
Series Designer: Alex Ferrari

Photo research by Connie Gardner

Cover photo by Age footstock/Pixtail

The photographs in this book are used by permission and through the courtesy of:
Corbis: Roy Morsch, 5; *Getty Images:* Stephen Simpson, 4; Visuals Unlimited, 9; Taxi, 11; Michael Newman,
12; Barbara Peacock, 13; Dann Tardif, 17; Sharie Kennedy, 19; Altrendo, 20; Seymour Hewitt, 21; Ben
Chernus, 23; Bernard Jolivait, 25; *PhotoResearchers:* Edward Kinsman, 15.

Printed in China
1 3 5 6 4 2

CONTENTS

OUCH! . . . 5

I DIDN'T CHOOSE TO GET THAT BRUISE . . . 7

YOU'VE SCRAPED YOUR SKIN . . . 14

EAT WELL TO STAY WELL . . . 18

SAFETY FIRST . . . 22

GLOSSARY . . . 27

FIND OUT MORE . . . 28

INDEX . . . 30

OUCH!

It's a great day! You can't wait to try out your new roller skates. You put them on and you're out the door.

What a feeling! It's like you're flying down the street. You're picking up speed now. That may be why you don't see the uneven break in the pavement. You hit it, and seconds later, you are flat on your face.

The fun is over and suddenly, everything hurts. Your knee and elbow are badly scraped but you make your way home. Your mother's

It may be fun and exciting, but skating too fast can end in a nasty fall with skin injuries.

◄ Elbows and knees are the most common places to scrape during a fall.

smile disappears when she sees you come through the door. "Let's get you taken care of," she says.

At this point, you feel both hurt and embarrassed. The scrapes on your knee and elbow really sting. You feel a bump forming on your forehead. You're sure that you'll have some bruises, too.

Then your mother says, "Don't worry, you're going to be fine. Anybody can have a fall."

You know she is right. You've had bumps, bruises, and scrapes before. Now you are reading a book about them. When you get to the last page, you'll understand how these injuries happen. You'll also know what you can do to get fewer of them. So keep reading and stay safe!

DID YOU KNOW?

Did you know that scrapes are among the most common skin injuries? Most scrapes occur during the warmer months when your arms and legs are less likely to be covered. Who gets the most scrapes? School-aged children between five and nine years old.

I Didn't Choose to Get That Bruise

Everyone knows what a bruise looks like. You've probably had bruises and have seen them on other kids. You can get bruised in lots of different ways.

It can happen when you're running through the living room. As you race past the coffee table, you might bang your knee. That can give you a bruise. You can also get a bruise from a fall. If you fell off your bike, it's likely that you'd be bruised.

Being hit with a hard object can give you a bruise as well. Let's say that you're up to bat in a baseball game. The pitcher is not having a good day. The ball doesn't come near the bat, but hits your leg instead. That can give you a bad bruise.

Have you ever gotten your fingers caught in a desk or dresser drawer? Maybe you were looking inside one when the phone rang. You quickly closed the drawer to run to get the phone. Oh, no! Your fingers were still inside. You can bet that your fingers would be bruised.

HOW BRUISES BEGIN

Bruises happen when your body's **soft tissues** are injured. When this occurs, some of the tiny **blood vessels** just beneath your skin break. As these vessels break, red blood cells escape from them. The blood stays at the site of the injury and forms a bruise.

If you've had bruises, you know they can be colorful. At first, the bruised area looks red and feels very tender. Then, in a few days, it turns a purplish blue color. This colorful area is actually the blood that leaked beneath your skin.

Yet the bruise does not stay that color for long. Within five to ten days, it turns a yellowish green. After that, the bruise becomes light brown. Then it just keeps getting lighter until it disappears.

The bruise disappears because your body heals itself. The broken vessels repair themselves so no more blood leaks out. The dead blood cells that formed the bruise break down into very small pieces. These pieces are taken away by fresh blood and tissue cells.

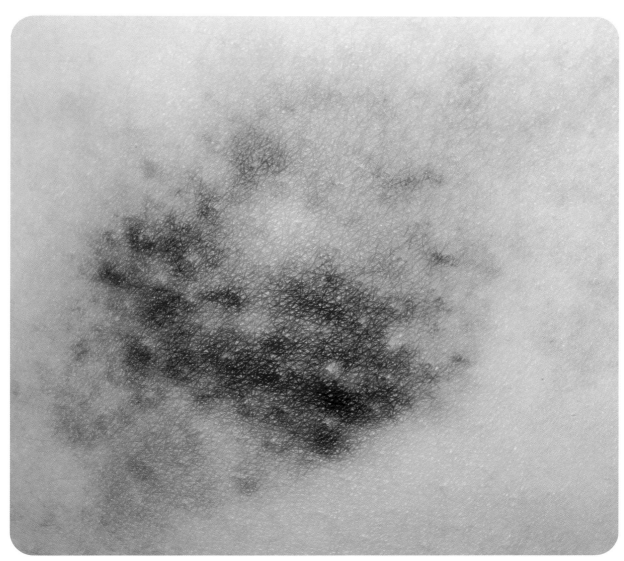

As bruises heal they change in color. This purplish yellow bruise is just a few days old.

BUMPS—THE BRUISE'S COUSIN

Sometimes when you bruise, a bump forms. These injuries often go together. That's why people sometimes call them cousins.

When a bump forms after an injury, blood from the broken blood vessels along with other fluid from the body collects there. Your skin swells so that the bump can form. The bump feels hard, and it is usually sore.

A bump may not look great, but it serves a purpose. It protects the hurt area as the body repairs itself. The additional blood that flowed to the spot also helps in the healing process.

Like bruises, bumps do not last very long. As your body heals, the bump shrinks.

Before long, it disappears just as a bruise does.

WHAT TO DO WHEN YOU GET A BRUISE, BUMP, OR BOTH

After you've been hurt, you will need to rest the injured part of your body. Wrap a cold pack or ice bag in a damp cloth. Then gently place it on the injured area. Do this for about twenty to thirty minutes every hour for the next twenty-four hours. It is also important to keep the injured part of your body raised.

The injured area around a bruise sometimes swells. This bump protects the hurt area as it heals.

The hurt area may be sore for a couple of days, so take it easy. Give yourself some time to rest and get better. Before you know it, you'll be ready to go again!

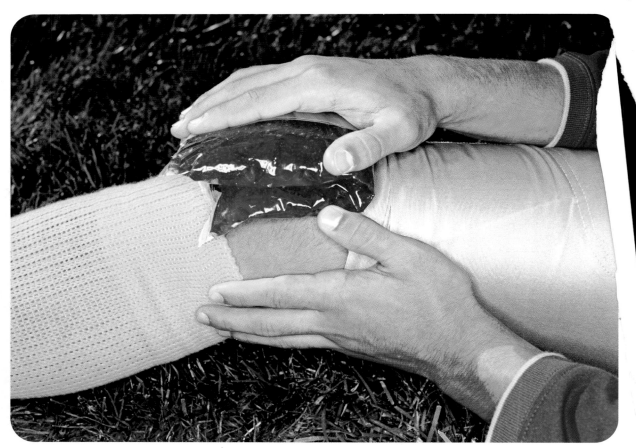

An ice bag helps bring down swelling to an injured area.

THE SKIN YOU'RE IN

Question: What's your body's largest **organ**?

Answer: It's not your heart, lungs, liver, or even your brain.

It's your skin!

You may not think of your skin as an organ, but it is.

Your skin is important. It keeps your insides inside your body. Your skin also protects you from germs. It helps control your body temperature, too. Take good care of your skin. Keep it clean and try not to bruise it.

You've Scraped Your Skin

You don't have to fall out of a tree to scrape your skin. It happens to kids all the time. Let's say you're home and you hear the doorbell ring. Your friend is coming over and you're sure that's him at the door. As you run to let him in, you trip and fall. You're not badly hurt, but you've scraped your knee.

JUST WHAT IS A SCRAPE, ANYWAY?

A scrape is a type of skin **wound**. With a scrape, some of the skin is rubbed or torn off. Even though scrapes are not as deep as cuts, they can really hurt. That's because scrapes are usually larger than cuts. They can cover a bigger area.

Sometimes you get scraped and don't bleed. That scrape

wasn't very deep. When there is bleeding, it means that the tiny blood vessels just beneath the skin have broken.

Soon this blood begins to stick together, or **clot**. This stops more blood and other body fluids from leaking out. Before long, the blood clot dries up and hardens. This forms a **scab** over the scraped area.

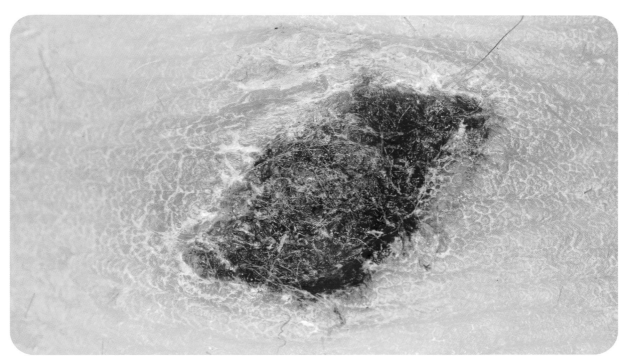

The hard scab that forms over a scrape protects the healing area and keeps germs out.

Be sure to have an adult help clean and bandage scrapes.

WHAT DO YOU DO FOR A SCRAPE?

If you scraped your skin, would you know what to do? If not, follow the steps below and you'll be fine.

MORE ABOUT SCRAPES

You can get a scrape anywhere. However, most scrapes occur on the hands, knees, elbows, **forearms**, and **shins**. Scrapes usually heal within five to fourteen days. You should see your doctor if your scrape does not heal in two weeks.

First, clean the wound. Rinse off the area and then wash it well with soap and warm water. Ask a responsible adult to help you with this. That person can make sure that the wound is completely clean. Next, apply an **antibiotic cream**. These creams help kill germs.

Cover a large or bloody scrape with a bandage. Change the bandage every day. Also be sure to change the bandage if it becomes wet or dirty.

Once a scab forms you won't need a bandage any longer. The scab acts as a barrier to keep out germs. Before long, the scab will fall off, and you'll be as good as new.

EAT WELL TO STAY WELL

Have you ever heard the saying, "You are what you eat?" A proper diet helps keep you healthy and strong. Eating well can also aid in the healing process. Some foods contain vitamins that can affect blood clotting. This is important when you bruise or scrape your skin.

HELP WITH HEALING

The vitamins A, C, and E (ACE) help keep your skin healthy as well as help it heal. Vitamin A is found in eggs, sweet potatoes, carrots, broccoli, mustard greens, zucchini, and other foods.

Do you like cantaloupe, oranges, and kiwis? These fruits contain lots of vitamin C. Vitamin E is found in margarine,

WHAT YOU EAT

How do you decide what to eat? When you are hungry or thirsty, do you reach for a package of gummy bears and a sugary soda? While this is a quick and easy snack, it might not be the best choice.

It is important to have a well-balanced diet. It should include meat, fish, eggs, cheese, or dried beans. Fruits and vegetables are good for you, too. There should also be some breads, cereals, crackers, rice, or pasta. Lastly, there's even room for a small amount of fats, oils, and sweets in your diet.

Oranges are loaded with vitamin C, which helps heal cuts and scrapes.

whole grains, vegetable oil, and olives.

Zinc can also be helpful in healing wounds. It is found in nuts, cheese, meat, and **grains**.

Eat right to feel right. You only have one body, so treat it well. No one wants to get any bumps, bruises, or scrapes. But if you do, eating right should help you make a speedy recovery.

HOW MUCH IS A SERVING?

In learning about a proper diet, you may often hear the term serving. It is used to let you know how much of a particular food you should eat. Do you know how much a serving is for different foods? Take the quiz below to see.

Question: You want to have a serving of spaghetti. Which of the choices below should you pick?

A. a full plate of spaghetti

B. a soup bowl of spaghetti

C. one half of one cup of spaghetti

The correct answer is C. If you answered A or B you might be eating too much spaghetti!

SAFETY FIRST

Question: What's better than healing from an injury?

Obvious answer: Not getting hurt to begin with.

Solution: With just a little extra care, you may be able to get less bumps, bruises, and scrapes.

Sometimes young people get hurt when they are out playing. If that's happened to you, you're not alone. Every year, over thirty million children in the United States play sports and anywhere from three to five million of these go to hospital emergency rooms.

PLAYING IT SAFE

It's great to have fun, but safety is important, too. You may be able to avoid many bumps, bruises, and scrapes by following some simple safety rules. The measures below will put you on the right track.

If you're going biking or horseback riding, be sure to wear a helmet. The same goes for skateboarding or rollerblading. Do you play baseball or softball? It's important to wear a batting helmet, shin guards, and elbow guards when you do.

Wearing protective gear when playing is always a good idea to help prevent injuries.

Other sports require different safety gear. Find out what you need to play safely. Learn how to use this equipment properly. Remember to wear this gear during practices as well as during games. Accidents can happen then, too.

When you're playing, always follow the rules of the game. Everyone needs to do this. When you know what to expect, you're less likely to get hurt.

If you're tired, don't force yourself to play. Try watching from the sidelines for a while. When you're tired you can get careless, and that's when accidents and injuries happen. It's also not a good idea to play if you're still healing after being hurt. Tell your coach or parents if an injury is still painful. Take the time you need to get better.

IT CAN HAPPEN AT HOME

Of course, you don't have to be out playing to get hurt. Many accidents happen at home. However, you can take steps to help keep both you and your family safe.

Start by remembering to put away your shoes, book bags, and toys. If these are in their proper place, no one can trip over them. Also keep scissors, arts and craft supplies with sharp edges, and other pointed items safely in boxes or draws.

An injury can happen even in your own bedroom! Keep it tidy to avoid tripping and hurting yourself.

Often scrapes result from bumping into these.

Bumps, bruises, and scrapes are usually not serious injuries. Yet they can hurt and make you pretty uncomfortable for a while. Hopefully, most of the time, you'll be able to avoid them. It's possible to have fun while staying safe. That's the best way to have fun!

GLOSSARY

antibiotic cream — a cream used to kill germs

blood vessels — the narrow tubes throughout your body through which your blood travels

clot — the process through which blood thickens and becomes more solid

forearm — the part of the arm extending from the elbow to the wrist

grains — cereal plants such as wheat or oats

organ — a part of the body that does a particular job

scab — the hard covering that forms over an injury as it heals

shin — the front of the leg between the knee and ankle

soft tissues — body tissues that connect, support, or surround other body parts. For example, muscle is soft tissue that supports bones.

wound — an injury in which the skin has been torn

FIND OUT MORE

BOOKS

Gray, Susan H. *The Skin*. Mankato, MN: Child's World, 2006.

Royston, Angela. *Bumps and Bruises*. Chicago: Heinemann Library, 2004.

———.*Why Do Bruises Change Color? and Other Questions*. Chicago: Heinemann Library, 2003.

Scott, Janine. *The Food Pyramid*. Minneapolis, MN: Compass Point Books, 2003.

Smithyman, Kathryn. *Active Kids*. New York: Crabtree, 2003.

DVDS

Danger Rangers: Wild Wheels. Big Kids Productions, 2006.

Safety on Wheels with The Safety Sarge. Customflix, 2006.

WEB SITES

Bikes & Wheel Sport Safety Kids Page

www.nysgtsc.state.ny.us/Kids/kid-bike.htm

Visit this Web site to learn how to stay safe when riding a bike or roller-skating. Don't miss the bike helmet coloring page or the safety jigsaw puzzle page.

MyPyramid for Kids

www.mypyramid.gov/

Check out this Web site for tips for healthy eating. Be sure to play the MyPyramid Blast Off Game.

INDEX

Page numbers in **boldface** are illustrations

antibiotic cream, 17, 27

blood clotting, 15, **15**, 18, 27
blood vessels, 8, 27
bruises, 8, **9**, 10, 12
bumps, 10, **11**

clots, blood, 15, **15,** 18, 27
cold packs, 10, **12**

diet, 18–21

first aid
    bumps and bruises, 12
   scrapes, 17
food, 18–21
forearm, 17, 27

grains, 20

home safety, 24, **25,** 26

ice bags, 10, **12**

organ, 13, 27

safety, 22–24, 26
scabs, 15, **15,** 17, 27
scrapes, 6, 14–17, **15**
shin, 17, 27
skin, 13
soft tissue, 8, 27
sports safety, 23–24

vitamins, 18, 20

wounds, 14, 27

zinc, 20

ABOUT THE AUTHOR

Award-winning author Elaine Landau has written over three hundred books for young readers. Many of these are on health and science topics.

Ms. Landau received her bachelor's degree in English and Journalism from New York University and a master's degree in Library and Information Science from Pratt Institute. You can visit Elaine Landau at her Web site: www.elainelandau.com.